YOU CAN
play harmonica

by Amy Appleby & Peter Pickow

To Ed Smith, Jerome Callet, and Stratosphere

Order No. AM 932350
US International Standard Book Number: 0.8256.1517.8
UK International Standard Book Number: 0.7119.5215.9

Exclusive Distributors:
Music Sales Corporation
257 Park Avenue South, New York, NY 10010 USA
Music Sales Limited
8/9 Frith Street, London W1V 5TZ England
Music Sales Pty. Limited
120 Rothschild Street, Rosebery, Sydney, NSW 2018, Australia

Printed and bound in the United States of America by
Vicks Lithograph and Printing

Amsco Publications
New York • London • Paris • Sydney

Compact Disc Track Listing

Table of Contents

Introduction

It's true. With a little study and practice, anyone can play harmonica—and this proven program will give you the chance to play in a variety of popular styles—including rock, blues, folk, and classical music. This easy, step-by-step method will guide you through all the basics of harp technique—and teach you all the skills you need to play hundreds of new songs on your own. You'll strengthen and develop these important playing skills in exciting performance sessions when you play the popular hits of Elvis Presley, Cat Stevens, the Beach Boys, and the Animals—as well as memorable tunes recorded by Robert Johnson, James Taylor, Judy Collins, and Ella Fitzgerald. Along the way, you'll learn a variety of professional solo techniques. These include traditional folk, pop, and classical techniques like tonguing, phrasing, and vibrato—as well as blues and rock moves like bending, sliding, shaking, and wah-wah.

A Little History

The harmonica (also called the *mouth harp* or *mouth organ*) is a *reed* or *wind instrument*. One form was invented in 1821 by F. Buschmann—and another early model (called the *Aeolina*) was invented in 1829 by Charles Wheatstone. During the 1830s, Matthias Hohner created another harmonica version, which most closely resembles the harmonicas used today.

The harmonica was introduced to America by German immigrants—and quickly gained acceptance throughout the country. The instrument was inexpensive and easy to play, as well as being portable and loud enough to be heard at concerts, dances, and singalongs. These factors made the harmonica a natural choice for people of all classes and backgrounds—and the instrument soon took its place in traditional folk bands as a natural complement to the fiddle, banjo, and guitar.

Early blues musicians found the harp perfectly suited to their earthy, soulful style. They developed a whole range of playing techniques which gave a strong new voice to this little German instrument. Since then, the harp has found a place in all styles of music from rock and pop to country and jazz.

Choosing a Harmonica

This book is designed to be used with a ten-hole harmonica in the key of C. This type of harp is called the *pocket harmonica* (as distinguished from the *chromatic harmonica*, which is favored by classical, modern jazz, and new age artists). The pocket harmonica is commonly used by folk, country, pop, blues, and rock players, including Bob Dylan, Charlie McCoy, Neil Young, James Cotton, Bruce Springsteen, and many others.

Even the best quality instruments get "played-out" after about six months of consistent playing—so it's a good idea to begin with a new or little-used C harmonica. If you do not already own an instrument, you'll find it easy to obtain one from your local music store—or through mail order. You'll be glad if you pay a little extra to get a quality brand harmonica. The lesser-quality instrument may be less expensive—but "you gets what you pays for."

Public health laws do not permit you to try out your instrument before you purchase it. Many music stores have a harmonica testing bellows—and will test the instrument for you. After you've bought the harp you want, you can test each note of the instrument, as described in the next section. Many harmonicas which appear to have a bum note or two will correct themselves after several hours of gentle playing. Take the instrument home and give it a good try (but don't be tempted to blow hard). If any notes still sound bad after you've played the instrument for a couple of days, take it back to the store and ask the salesperson if it's possible to get a replacement. They may offer you a replacement on the spot, or provide you with the manufacturer's address so you can return it with a note indicating which holes do not play.

Getting Started

The airholes of the *mouthpiece* are numbered one through ten—and each airhole houses two reeds. One reed vibrates when air is blown through the hole (↑)—the other, when air is drawn through the hole (↓). So, with its ten holes, the harmonica produces twenty notes.

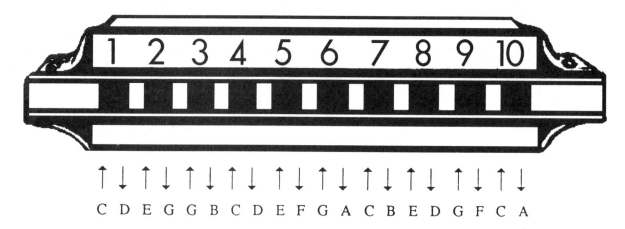

Hold the harmonica firmly in your left hand as you would a sandwich (the instrument is often affectionately called the "tin sandwich" or "chrome sandwich"). You'll be using your right hand later to achieve special playing effects such as vibrato, fanning, muting, and wah-wah. For now, hold it in your left hand with the holes facing you—and the number **1** hole at your left.

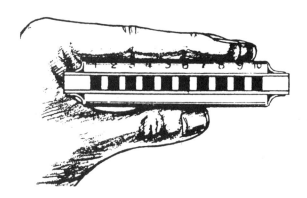

Shape your mouth into a small "o" about the size of one of the instrument's airholes.

Mouth Position for Single Notes

Now play the twenty notes of the C harmonica as shown in the diagram below. Airhole numbers are circled to indicate an inhaled breath (or *draw*) and uncircled for an exhaled breath (or *blow.*). Gently blow, then draw on each airhole in sequence, beginning with the lowest note (airhole 1). Be sure to keep the moist inside of your puckered lips gently pressed against the mouthpiece of the instrument.

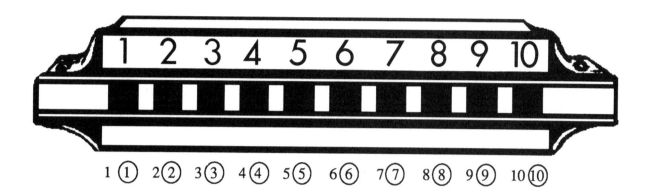

If any notes sound weak, fuzzy, or off-pitch, adjust your mouth position on the airhole or reshape the small "o" formed by your lips. Don't worry if you find it a bit difficult to play the draw note on airhole 2—this same note may be played by blowing airhole 3. Harp manufacturers have adapted the draw reed in airhole 2 somewhat for note bending, as you will see when you get the "Special Effects."

Harmonica Care

Most name-brand pocket harmonicas come in a case. If your harp doesn't have a case (or if the case becomes damaged with use), store the instrument in a plastic bag or lint-free pouch or box. Protecting your instrument from dust and other foreign matter will definitely prolong its life. Remember to rinse any food particles from your mouth before your play your instrument. After playing, tap the hole side of the harp against your palm or thigh to remove any particles or excess moisture.

There's no need to soak your instrument in water (or beer) after you buy it, as some old-timers suggest. This process only works for harps manufactured with a wooden body. The liquid swells the wood and causes a tighter seal between the body and the metal plates. Soaking can increase the volume of a wooden-bodied harp—and may cure any notes that aren't blowing true. However, these benefits are often only temporary—the wood shrinks after time and new gaps inevitably form. In the long run, soaking can rust the instrument's metal reeds, weaken the wooden body—and considerably shorten the life of your instrument. However, if you have a wooden-bodied harmonica that is on its last legs, you might try soaking it before you discard it. This could give your instrument a few more weeks of playing life. Simply soak the harp in water for an hour or two, then tap out any excess water and give it a try.

Straight Harp

Straight harp is the easiest harmonica playing style. For this basic style, you use a C harmonica to play tunes in the key of C Major. Straight-harp playing is also sometimes called *first-position* playing. Bob Dylan, Woody Guthrie, and Charlie McCoy have created many memorable recordings in this playing style. Once you've mastered first position, it's easy to move on to the more advanced playing positions of blues and rock.

Three-Note Chords

The harmonica is designed to provide chord accompaniment, as well as solo lines. Playing chords (or *chording*) is the easiest straight-harp playing technique. A *chord* is simply a group of notes that are played together. A three-note chord is called a *triad*. To play a three-note chord, shape your mouth into an oval the size of three airholes.

Mouth Position for Three-Note Chords

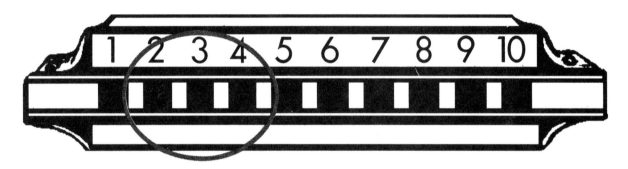

Now practice these three-note chords in sequence, beginning with airholes 2, 3, and 4. Remember, circled chords indicate air is drawn through airholes, while uncircled chords are played by blowing.

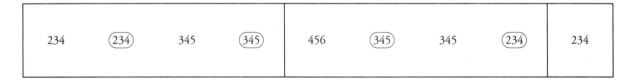

234	(234)	345	(345)	456	(345)	345	(234)	234

Now play the well-known ballad "Long, Long Ago" using three-note chords throughout. Each group of three numbers represents the three airholes used for a given chord.

Long, Long Ago

Tell	me	the	tales	that	to	me	were	so	dear,
234	234	(234)	345	345	(345)	456	(456)	456	345

Long,	long	a	-	go,		Long.	long	a	-	go,
456	(345)	345		(234)		(345)	345	(234)		234

Sing	me	the	songs	I	de -	light	- ed	to	hear,
234	234	(234)	345	345	(345)	456	(456)	456	345

Long,	long	a	-	go,	long	a	-	go.
456	(345)	345		(234)	345	(234)		234

Now	you	are	come,	all	my	grief	is	re	- moved,
456	(345)	345	(234)	(123)	(123)	(345)	345	(234)	234

Let	me	for	- get	that	so	long	you	have	roved,
456	(345)	345	(234)	(123)	(123)	(345)	345	(234)	234

Let	me	be	- lieve	that	you	love	as	you	loved,
234	234	(234)	345	345	(345)	456	(456)	456	345

Long,	long	a	-	go,	long	a	-	go.
456	(345)	345		(234)	345	(234)		234

Two-Note Chords

Playing a two-note chord is just like playing a three-note chord—just form your lips into a smaller oval (the size of two airholes, as shown).

Mouth Position for Two-Note Chords

Now get ready to play "Down in the Valley." This arrangement uses a two-note chord at the beginning of the second and fourth lines where three-note chords are not possible (because you run out of notes). You often need to mix two- and three-note chords in this way during a song to achieve the best sound. The high note of each chord provides the melody for this classic folk waltz. Practice "Down in the Valley" until you can play it smoothly in tempo.

Down in the Valley

Down	in	the	val -	ley,	the	val -	ley	so	low,		
123	234	(234)	345	234	345	345	(234)	234	(234)		

Hang	your	head	o -	ver,		hear	the	wind	blow.		
(12)	(123)	(234)	(345)	(234)		(123)	234	(234)	234		

Hear	the	wind	blow,	dear,		hear	the	wind	blow,		
123	234	(234)	345	234		345	(234)	234	(234)		

Hang	your	head	o -	ver,		hear	the	wind	blow.		
(12)	(123)	(234)	(345)	(234)		(123)	234	(234)	234		

Playing in Thirds

Many song melodies may be played using two-note chords throughout the song. This harp technique is also known as *playing in thirds,* because most two-note chords form an *interval* called a *harmonic third.*

Place your mouth over airholes 3 and 4, and practice this two-note exercise using alternating blow and draw chords.

34	(34)	45	(45)	56	(45)	45	(34)	34

Now play this two-note exercise using blow chords, then draw chords.

34	45	56	45	34		(34)	(45)	(56)	(45)	(34)

Now play the folk favorite "Kumbaya" using two-note chords throughout. Play the song twice and then finish up with the special ending provided.

Kumbaya

Kum - bay -	ya,	my	Lord,	Kum - bay -	ya.
34 45	56	56	56	(56) (56)	56

Kum - bay -	ya,	my	Lord,	Kum - bay -	ya.
34 45	56	56	56	(45) 45	(34)

Kum - bay -	ya,	my	Lord,	Kum - bay -	ya.
34 45	56	56	56	(56) (56)	56

Oh,	Lord,	Kum -	bay -	ya.	
(45)	45 34	(34)	(34)	34	*repeat*

ending

Kum - bay -	ya.	
(34) (45)	56	

Now play "Clementine" using two-note chords for the verse section—and three-note chords during the chorus.

Clementine

In	a	cav - ern,	in	a	can - yon,	ex - ca -	vat - ing	for	a	mine,
34	34	34	23	45	45	45	34	34	45	56	56	④⑤	45	㉞

Lived	a	min - er,	for - ty -	nin - er,	and	his	daugh - ter,	Cle - men -	tine.
㉞	45	㊸	㊸	45	㉞	45	34	34	45	㉞	⑫	㉓	㉞	34

Oh	my	dar - ling,	oh	my	dar - ling,	oh	my	dar - ling,	Cle - men -	tine,
234	234	234	123	345	345	345	234	234	345	456	456	③④⑤	345	②③④

You	are	lost	and	gone	for -	ev - er;	dread - ful	sor - ry,	Cle - men -	tine.
②③④	345	③④⑤	③④⑤	345	②③④	345	234	234	345	②③④	⑫	①②③	②③④	234

Tonguing

Tonguing is a technique used by all wind instrument players to separate and articulate individual notes of a song. To tongue a note, the harpist lightly whispers the word "too" as the note is played. Try saying the word "too" in an unvoiced whisper as you exhale—then whisper "too" as you inhale. Now get a good breath and place your mouth over airholes 456. Try tonguing eight times on the blow chord and eight times on the draw chord, as indicated.

too	too	too	too	too	too	too	too	too	too	too	too	too	too	too	too
456	456	456	456	456	456	456	456	④⑤⑥	④⑤⑥	④⑤⑥	④⑤⑥	④⑤⑥	④⑤⑥	④⑤⑥	④⑤⑥

Professional harpists use tonguing to add clarity and control to their performance. This technique is particularly important when the same note is repeated in a song, as in "Jingle Bells." Practice this tune until you can play it accurately from memory.

Jingle Bells

Jin	-	gle	bells,		jin	-	gle	bells,			jin	-	gle	all	the	way.
345		345	345		345		345	345			345		456	234	(234)	345

Oh,	what	fun	it		is	to	ride	in	a		one	-	horse	o	-	pen	sleigh.
(45)	(45)	(45)	(45)		(45)	45	45	45	45		45		(34)	(34)		45	(34)

Jin	-	gle	bells,		jin	-	gle	bells,			jin	-	gle	all	the	way.
345		345	345		345		345	345			345		456	234	(234)	345

Oh,	what	fun	it		is	to	ride	in	a		one	-	horse	o	-	pen	sleigh.
(45)	(45)	(45)	(45)		(45)	45	45	45	45		56		56	(45)		(34)	234

Four-Note Chords

Some songs may be played using four-note chords. For this chording technique, shape your mouth into a large oval the size of four airholes.

Mouth Position for Four-Note Chords

Now play the familiar lullaby "Hush, Little Baby," using the indicated two-note, three-note, and four-note chords. Use tonguing to clarify each chord.

Hush, Little Baby

Hush,		lit	-	tle		ba	-	by,		don't	say	a	word.
123		2345		2345		2345		(2345)		2345	(1234)	(1234)	(1234)

Dad	-	dy's		gon	-	na	buy	you	a	mock	-	ing	-	bird.	And,
(12)		(1234)		(1234)		(1234)	(1234)	(1234)	2345	(1234)		1234		1234	123

if		that		mock	-	ing	-	bird	don't	sing,
123		2345		2345		(2345)		2345	(1234)	(1234)

Dad	-	dy's		gon	-	na	buy	you	a	dia	-	mond	ring.
(12)		(1234)		(1234)		(1234)	(1234)	(1234)	2345	(1234)		1234	1234

Single Noting

Now that you've learned some chording techniques, try playing some single-note melody lines. Shape your mouth into a small "o" the size of one airhole.

Practice this exercise until you can play it evenly and smoothly. Here are some things to remember as you play.

- Form a firm seal with your lips against the instrument mouthpiece.
- Inhale and exhale evenly so that the notes sound smooth and connected.
- Move the instrument rather than your mouth as you change airholes.

4	(4)	5	(5)	6	(5)	5	(4)	4

Now play the melody of "Michael, Row the Boat Ashore," a folk favorite which was a number one hit for the Highwaymen in 1961.

Michael, Row the Boat Ashore

Mich - ael,	row	the	boat	a -	shore,	Hal - le -	lu -	jah,
4　5	6	5	6	⑥	6　5	6	⑥	6

Mich - ael,	row	the	boat	a -	shore,	Hal - le -	lu -	jah.
5　6	6	5	⑤ 5		④ 4	④	5 ④	4

Sis - ter,	help	to	trim	the	sails,	Hal - le -	lu -	jah,
4　5	6	5	6	⑥	6　5	6	⑥	6

Sis - ter,	help	to	trim	the	sails.	Hal - le -	lu -	jah.
5　6	6	5	⑤ 5		④ 4	④	5 ④	4

The High Range

Now let's take a look at the high notes of the harp—and how to get the best results in this range. The pure and sweet quality of this range is well suited for straight-harp solos. Although it takes a little less breath to play high notes on the harp, it takes a little extra accuracy and control to get them sounding sweet.

First play the notes in the high range in sequence, beginning with the C note. Don't worry if this scale sounds a bit odd—the notes in the high range do not correspond with a typical scale pattern.

4 ④ 5 ⑤	6 ⑥ ⑦ 7	⑧ 8 ⑨ 9	⑩ 10 ⑩ 9	⑨ 8 ⑧ 7	⑦ ⑥ 6 ⑤	5 ④ 4

Skipping is an important playing technique that you'll use in many songs. The term simply means that you must skip over an airhole to get to the next note. This is accomplished by moving the harp quickly past the skipped airhole without sounding it. Try this technique in the following exercise.

8 6 8 6	⑧ ⑥ ⑧ ⑥	8 ⑥ 8 ⑥	⑧ 6 ⑧ 6	7

Now take a look at "Aura Lee," a beautiful ballad composed by George R. Poulton which has long been considered one of America's most popular love melodies. This moving song enjoyed a smash revival in 1956 when Elvis Presley recorded it as "Love Me Tender." This chart-busting hit was the title song for Elvis's first movie—and stayed in the number one position on the charts for five weeks. This popular tune made it back on the charts when Richard Chamberlain recorded it in 1962—and Percy Sledge, in 1967. Play this beautiful love song in the harmonica's high range.

Aura Lee (Love Me Tender)

As	the	black -	bird	in	the	spring	'Neath	the	wil -	low	tree.
6	7	⑦	7	⑧	⑥	⑧	7	⑦	⑥	⑦	7

Sat	and	piped,	I	heard	him	sing	Sing	of	Aur -	a	Lee.
6	7	⑦	7	⑧	⑥	⑧	7	⑦	⑥	⑦	7

Aur -	a	Lee,	Aur -	a	Lee,	Maid	of	gold -	en	hair,
8	8	8	8	8	8	8	⑧	7	⑧	8

Sun -	shine	came	a -	long	with	thee,	and	swal -	lows	in	the	air.
8	8	⑨	8	⑧	⑥	⑧	7	7	⑦	8	⑧	7

Breathing

Breath control is an essential part of playing any wind instrument. In this section, you'll learn breathing techniques that will give you stamina and help you add power to your harmonica playing.

All professional harp players use a technique called *deep breathing* or *diaphragmatic breathing* when they play. The *diaphragm* is a muscular plate that separates the chest cavity from the abdominal cavity. If you are fully supporting your voice, you will feel your diaphragm lower when you take a breath, as shown in the diagram.

Front View of Lungs With Diaphragm

--- = diaphragm when lower lungs are not filled with air

— = diaphragm when lower lungs are filled with air

As you take in breath, you should also feel your rib cage and abdomen expand, as shown.

Side View of Body

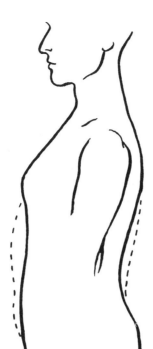

The dotted lines show the expansion of the rib cage when the lower lungs are filled with air.

When you exhale, you should feel your diaphragm raise, and your rib cage and abdomen return to normal size. A good harp player knows how to exhale fully, naturally, and smoothly when needed.

Unlike many other wind instruments, the harmonica is played by exhaling *and* inhaling. This means that it is possible to continue playing for long periods of time without stopping to take a breath. To see how this works, try playing "Tom Dooley" in the high range without pausing for breath.

Tom Dooley

Hang	down	your	head,	Tom	Doo	-	ley,
6	6	6	⑥	7	8		8

Hang	down	your	head,	and	cry.
6	6	6	⑥	7	⑧

Hang	down	your	head,	Tom	Doo	-	ley,
6	6	6	⑥	7	⑧		⑧

Poor	boy,	you're	bound	to	die.
⑧	⑧	8	7	⑥	7

Music Notation

Most sheet music does not feature harmonica tablature—so it pays to be able to read standard music notation if you want to learn new songs from the printed page. Once you are familiar with the notes of the harp, you'll be able to "play by ear," but even so, you'll find that being able to read music a little will come in very handy throughout your performance career.

Written music is a universal language of notes and symbols, arranged on the *staff* which consists of five lines and four spaces. The sign at the beginning of this staff is known as a *treble clef.* This clef is also called the *G clef,* because it curls around the second line of the staff—the position of the G note. This note serves as a point of reference for naming all other notes on the staff. Take another look at the twenty notes on the C harp, notated here in harmonica tablature and standard music notation.

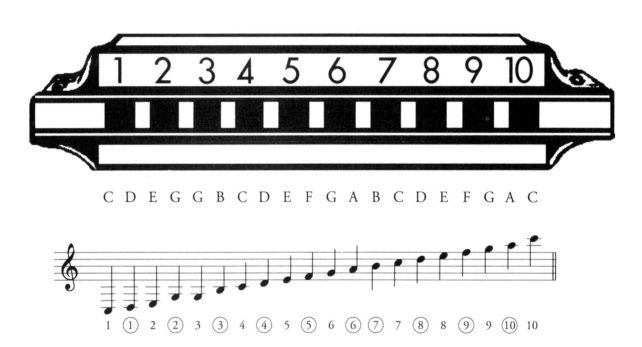

Note Values

Each note written on the staff not only tells you which note (or *pitch*) to play on the harmonica—but also how long the tone should last. The combined *note values* of a song melody form its *rhythm.* The basic unit of rhythm in music is called a *beat.* Musical notes range in length from just a fraction of a beat to a duration of several beats. Familiarize yourself with the duration in beats of each of these basic note values. Notice how the notes are distinguished by the presence or absence of a line or *stem*—and by appearance of the dot (or *notehead*), which may be either outlined or filled in. Take the time to memorize these different notes and their values.

o   **Whole Note** = 4 beats

𝅗𝅥   **Half Note** = 2 beats

♩   **Quarter Note** = 1 beat

♪   **Eighth Note** = 1/2 beat

♬   **Sixteenth Note** = 1/4 beat

Common Time

One important key to the overall rhythm of a piece is the *time signature,* a numerical symbol which appears after the clef at the beginning of a piece of music, as shown. This time signature indicates that the piece is written in $\frac{4}{4}$ *time* (pronounced "four-four time"), also called *common time* or *march time.* The top number (4) indicates that there are four beats per measure—and the bottom number (4) indicates that a quarter note gets one beat. Sometimes the symbol **C** is used to indicate $\frac{4}{4}$ time.

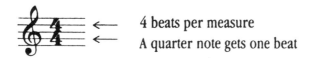 ← 4 beats per measure
← A quarter note gets one beat

Take a look at "Jingle Bells," which is written in common time. *Barlines* divide each *bar* (or *measure*) of the melody phrase into four equal beats (counted "**1**-2-**3**-4, **1**-2-**3**-4," and so on—with a stress on the first and third beat of each measure). A *double barline* marks the end of the excerpt. Play this single-note version of "Jingle Bells," shown here in harmonica tablature and standard music notation.

Jingle Bells

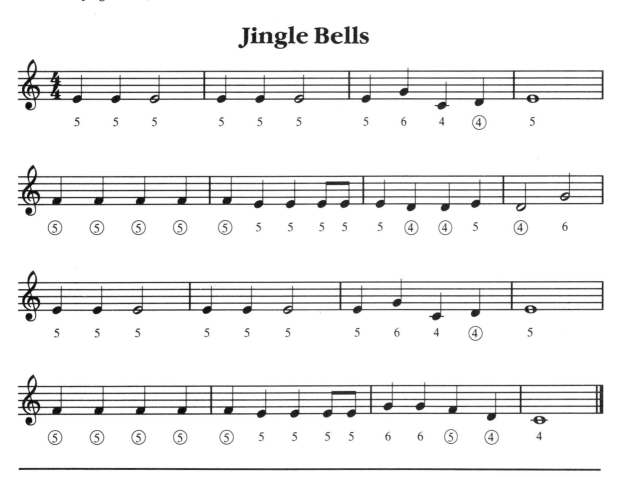

Rests

Most music is composed of sounds and silences. The silent beats in music are represented by signs called *rests*. Rests are named and valued in correspondence with the note values you learned previously.

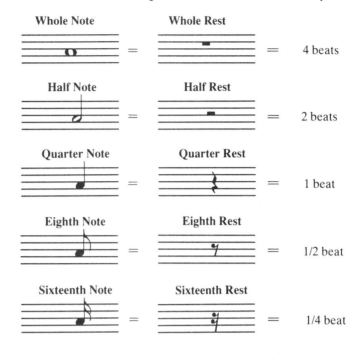

Whole Note	Whole Rest	
		4 beats
Half Note	Half Rest	
		2 beats
Quarter Note	Quarter Rest	
		1 beat
Eighth Note	Eighth Rest	
		1/2 beat
Sixteenth Note	Sixteenth Rest	
		1/4 beat

Rests and notes may be combined in the same measure, as long as their combined values add up to the correct number of beats. "Camptown Races" is written in common time, with four beats in every measure. As you play this lively tune, be sure to allow the appropriate number of silent beats where the rests occur in the melody. The two dots before the first double barline in this song form a *repeat sign*. When you reach this sign, go back to the beginning and repeat the section before going on.

Camptown Races

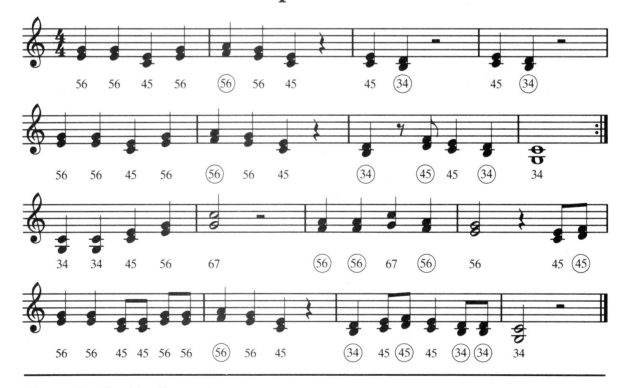

Waltz Time

Many songs are written in $\frac{3}{4}$ *time* ("three-four time")—also called *waltz time*—with three beats to a measure.

As you play "Drink to Me Only With Thine Eyes," put a slight stress on the first beat of every measure to accentuate the waltz feel. Notice that in $\frac{3}{4}$ time, the whole rest has a duration of three beats (not four beats, as in $\frac{4}{4}$ time). Just remember that a whole rest lasts for the "whole" measure, regardless of the time signature. For this reason, it is sometimes called a *measure rest*.

Drink to Me Only With Thine Eyes

Double Tonguing

Double tonguing is used to separate individual notes in an uptempo song. This technique is particularly important when the same note is repeated several times in a row. To double tongue a sequence of two notes, the harpist lightly whispers the syllables "too-koo" while playing. Try saying the syllables "too-koo" in an unvoiced whisper as you exhale—then whisper this phrase as you inhale. Now get a good breath, place your mouth over the 4,5, and 6 airholes, and use double tonguing to play this sequence of sixteenth notes, as shown. (Remember, four sixteenth-notes equal one beat.)

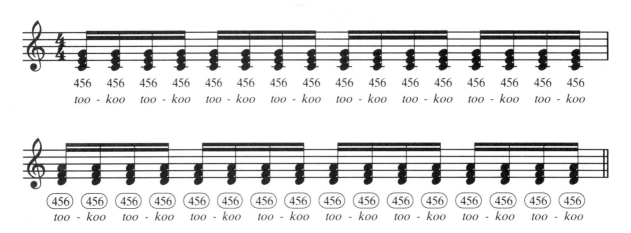

Now play "Polly Wolly Doodle" using tonguing and double tonguing where indicated. These techniques add speed and clarity to your playing—and will become second nature to you as you learn more and more songs. This one is in $\frac{2}{4}$ time, with two beats in each measure.

Polly Wolly Doodle

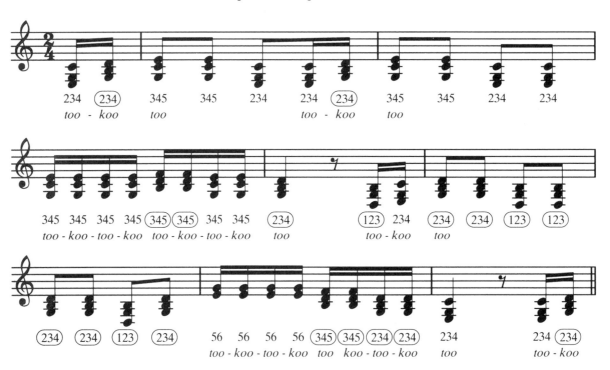

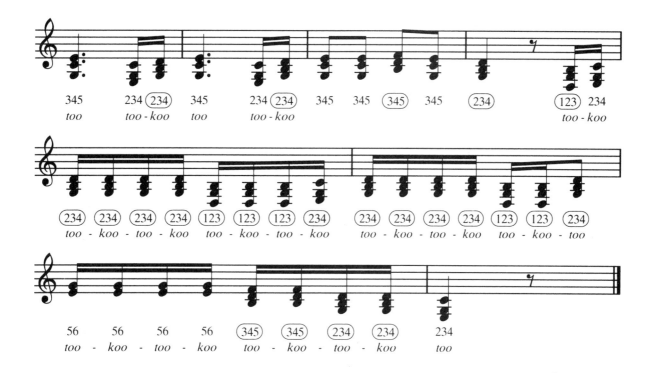

345   234 (234)   345   234 (234)   345   345   (345)   345   (234)   (123) 234

too   *too - koo*   *too*   *too - koo*   *too - koo*

(234) (234) (234) (234) (123) (123) (123) (234)   (234) (234) (234) (234) (123) (123) (234)

too - koo - too - koo   too - koo - too - koo   too - koo - too - koo   too - koo - too

56   56   56   56   (345)   (345)   (234)   (234)   234

too - koo - too - koo   too - koo - too - koo   too

Dotted Note Values

A dot placed after any note means that it should last one-and-a-half times its normal duration. For example, if you add a dot after a half note (which normally lasts for two beats), you get a *dotted half note*, which lasts three beats.

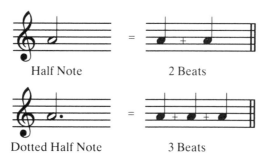

When a dot is placed after a quarter note (which normally lasts one beat), a *dotted quarter note* results—which lasts for one-and-a-half beats.

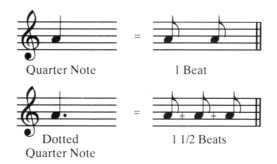

Dotted notes play an important role in the melody of "Silent Night," which is also in $\frac{3}{4}$ *time* (or *waltz time*). Work to make this one sound smooth and sweet in your instrument's high range.

Silent Night

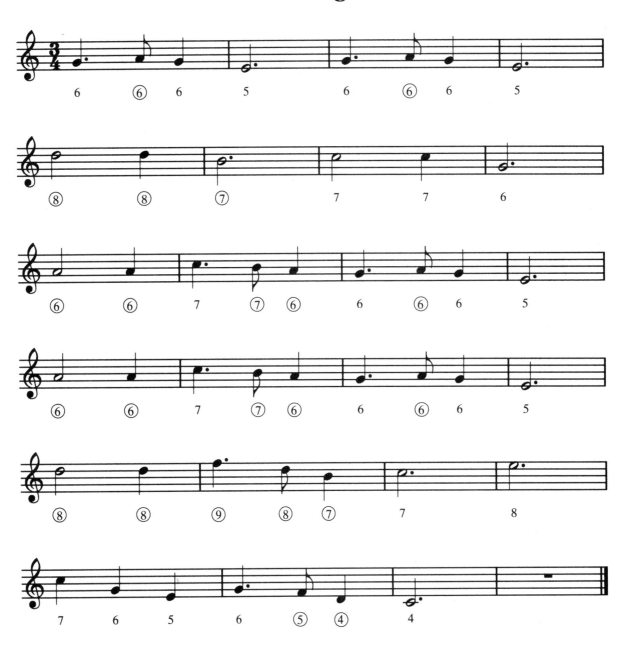

An eighth note is normally worth one-half beat—so a *dotted eighth note* lasts for three-quarters of a beat.

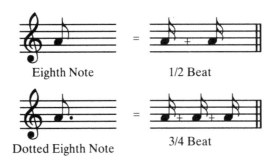

Eighth Note = 1/2 Beat

Dotted Eighth Note = 3/4 Beat

The dotted eighth note is often paired with a sixteenth note to create one full beat. This and other dotted rhythms create a lilting quality in "Simple Gifts," the haunting Shaker hymn made popular by Judy Collins during the seventies.

Simple Gifts

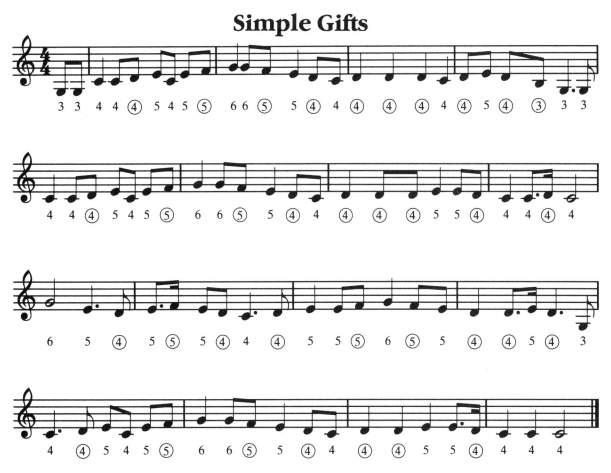

3 3 4 4 ④ 5 4 5 ⑤ 6 6 ⑤ 5 ④ 4 ④ ④ ④ 4 ④ 5 ④ ③ 3 3

4 4 ④ 5 4 5 ⑤ 6 6 ⑤ 5 ④ 4 ④ ④ ④ 5 5 ④ 4 4 ④ 4

6 5 ④ 5 ⑤ 5 ④ 4 ④ 5 5 ⑤ 6 ⑤ 5 ④ ④ 5 ④ 3

4 ④ 5 4 5 ⑤ 6 6 ⑤ 5 ④ 4 ④ ④ 5 5 ④ 4 4 4

Triplets

Composers and arrangers sometimes need to divide a basic note value into three notes of equal value. These three notes are collectively called a *triplet,* which is indicated by the numeral *3* above the notes.

A quarter-note triplet normally lasts for two beats—and is notated with a numeral *3* within a bracket. (The "quarter notes" in this triplet are actually each worth two-thirds of a beat.)

An eighth-note triplet normally lasts one beat—and is notated with a numeral *3* above the *beam* that links the three notes together. (The "eighth-notes" in this triplet are each worth one-third of one beat.)

Triplets add a certain stately beauty to the powerful hymn, "Amazing Grace." As a tribute to the lasting popularity of this song, Judy Collins made it a top-40 hit in 1971. The following year, the Royal Scots Dragoon Guards of Scotland's armored regiment recorded a bagpipe band version of this tune that put it back on the pop charts. Play this one in the high range at a slow tempo.

Amazing Grace

6 7 7 8 ⑧ 7 8 ⑧ 7 ⑥ 6 6 7

7 8 ⑧ 7 8 ⑧ 8 9 8 9

9 8 ⑧ 7 8 ⑧ 7 ⑥ 6 6 7

7 8 ⑧ 7 8 ⑧ 7

Ties

A *tie* is a curved line which links two or more notes of the same pitch. This indicates that a tone be held for the combined length of the two tied notes. In this arrangement of Peter, Paul, and Mary's folk song "Stewball," the first tie links a half note to a dotted half note—so hold this tone for five beats. The second tie links two dotted half notes—so hold this tone for six beats.

Stewball

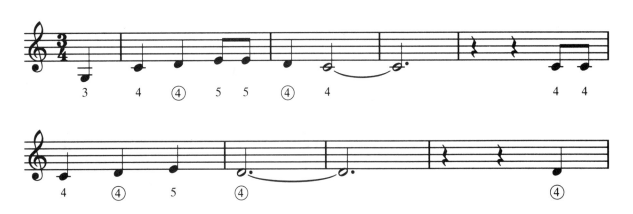

3 4 ④ 5 5 ④ 4 4 4

4 ④ 5 ④ ④

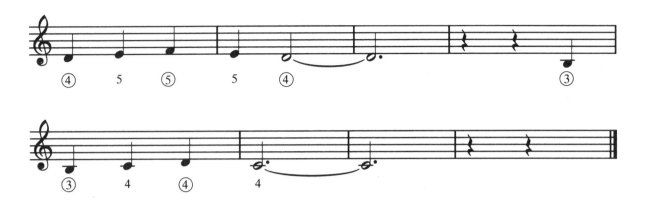

Legato and Staccato

A *slur* is a curved line connecting two or more notes of varying pitch. This mark indicates that the notes be played *legato*—that is, smoothly, without tonguing. Because of their similar appearance, ties are often confused with slurs. The way to tell them apart is to remember that ties link notes of the same pitch, while slurs always link notes of varying pitch. The slur in the first phrase of "Goodnight Ladies" means that you should not tongue the indicated notes.

A *staccato mark* appears as a dot above or below a note, as in the second measure of "Goodnight Ladies." This symbol tells you to tongue the note with a short, light accent. This provides an interesting contrast with the smooth legato playing in the first measure. Decide where you want to use staccato and legato playing when you are learning a new song. Then, pencil in these markings to remind you of your personal interpretation. Play this song now using legato and staccato playing where indicated.

Goodnight Ladies

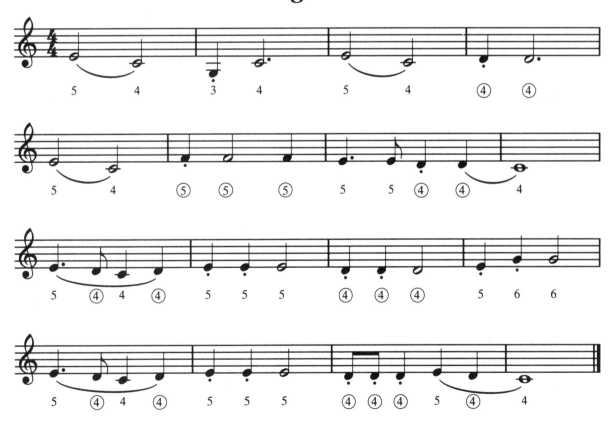

Adapting the Melody

As you've probably already discovered, it's sometimes necessary to adapt a melody in order to play it well on the C harmonica. That's because the twenty notes of the pocket harp don't always cover all the notes in a given tune (particularly if it contains sharps and flats). To see how this works, take a look at the first line of the classic ballad "Danny Boy." It is possible to play the low A note at the end of this phrase by *bending* the draw note on hole 3. (You will learn about bending in the "Special Effects" section.)

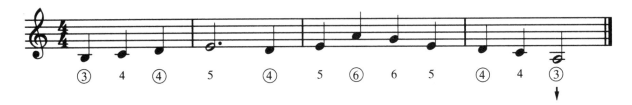

While this bent note may be perfect for the blues, it often sounds out of place in a straight-harp song. To avoid the A note, you might adapt the melody a bit and simply repeat the C note at the end of the phrase. This change works well because the C and A notes are both *chord tones* of the F Major triad, which provides the harmony in this measure. So you can see that it's helpful to know the chords of a song when you need to adapt the melody. This arrangement of "Danny Boy" features the C, G7, and F chords, indicated by *chord symbols* over the melody.

Now play "Danny Boy," which features several melody adaptations.

Danny Boy

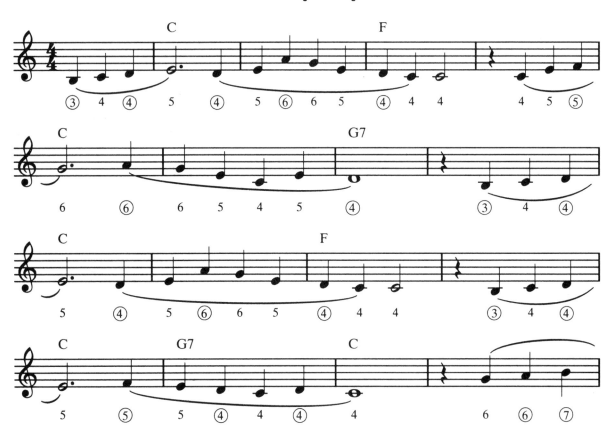

Countermelody

Soloists often create a second melody to a song—called a *countermelody* or *obligato*. This technique is effective in both solo and accompaniment parts. Whenever you feel like doing a little creative practice, try to write your own countermelody to a tune you already know. You'll find that some songs make good natural subjects for countermelody, while others do not. In the music for "Molly Malone," the melody is written on the top staff, and a countermelody is written on a bottom staff. If you examine these lines closely, you'll see that they are both based on the tones of the chords used in the song. Melody (or countermelody) notes that are not found in the chord used in a given measure of the song are called *passing tones*, because they quickly pass from one chord tone to another.

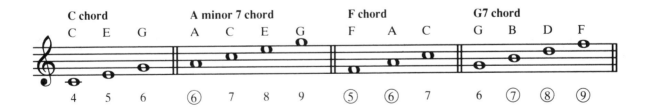

Play the melody of "Molly Malone," then go back to the beginning and play the countermelody. Once you can play both lines from memory, take the time to create your own original countermelody based on the song's chords. Write your countermelody down on paper once you've got it worked out.

Molly Malone

Special Effects

Professional harpists use quite a few different special effects to make their playing rich and interesting. In the sections that follow, you'll learn important techniques like vibrato, sliding, shaking, trilling, tongue blocking, and note bending. These effects will come in handy when you start playing blues and rock harp in later sections, where you'll learn additional special effects, including throat popping, wah-wah, and train sounds.

Vibrato

Vibrato is an important technique used by harmonica players to add character and feeling to a solo. Using the right hand as a mute, the player creates added vibrations on certain notes of a song. The resulting vibrato tones help add a mournful, tremulous sound to a song, particularly if the song is slow and sad.

Cup your right hand behind your left hand.

Vibrato Hand Position 1

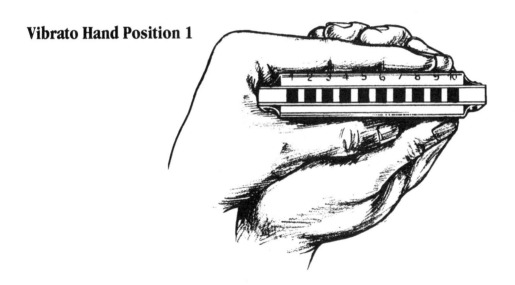

Now blow airholes 456 as you flutter the fingers of your cupped right hand, as shown.

Vibrato Hand Position 2

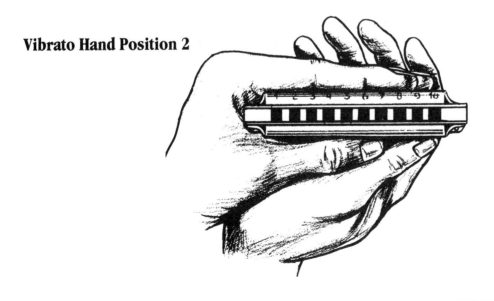

You'll find that your vibrato can be accentuated by forming a tight seal between your two cupped hands. The quality of the vibrato is also affected by the speed and steadiness of your right-hand finger movements. Play "Banks of the Ohio" using vibrato where indicated.

The Banks of the Ohio

Sliding

A well-placed *slide* can add character and energy to a harmonica solo. This technique is often used in uptempo songs. Place your mouth lightly on the 123 airholes of the harmonica. As you blow this chord, move the harmonica quickly to the left until your mouth is positioned on the 456 airholes, as indicated by the straight lines. Practice this chord slide four times.

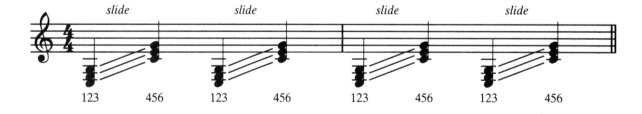

Now play "Oh, Susanna," which features this slide in the chorus. As you become more advanced, you'll see how slides can add much to blues solos.

Oh, Susanna

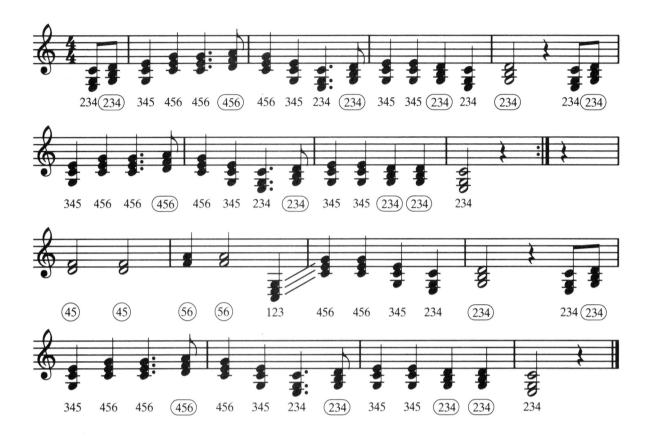

234 (234) 345 456 456 (456) 456 345 234 (234) 345 345 (234) 234 (234) 234 (234)

345 456 456 (456) 456 345 234 (234) 345 345 (234) (234) 234

(45) (45) (56) (56) 123 456 456 345 234 (234) 234 (234)

345 456 456 (456) 456 345 234 (234) 345 345 (234) (234) 234

Grace Note

A *grace note* is a quick, single note which serves as a melody decoration. The grace note is indicated in music by a small note which is joined to a melody note by a small slur. Place your mouth over airhole 6. Play the draw note on this airhole, then move the instrument quickly up to airhole 7 and back to 6 again. Practice this move until you can play it smoothly and naturally.

⑥ ⑦ ⑥ 6

Now play "Morning Has Broken," the beautiful hymn that Cat Stevens recorded as a pop hit in 1972. The grace notes which occur throughout this arrangement of the song give it a lovely, haunting quality.

Morning Has Broken

Double Grace Note

The *double grace note* is another effective ornament, which is sometimes called a *single shake.* As you'll learn in the next section, shaking is a valuable effect in both blues and straight-harp arrangements. Practice this ornament using two-note chords by first placing your mouth over airholes 4 and 5. As you blow this two-note chord, move the instrument quickly up to airholes 5 and 6, then back again. Then try the same move on the draw chord on holes 3 and 4.

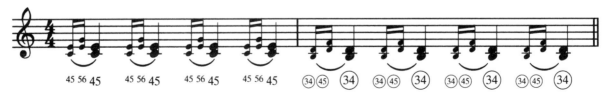

Now play "For He's a Jolly Good Fellow" using double grace notes where indicated. This ornament adds an energetic, jaunty sound to this old song. Although the time signature $\frac{6}{8}$ means "six beats per measure, eighth note gets one beat," songs written in $\frac{6}{8}$ are usually counted "in two." This means that a dotted quarter note would receive one beat, and groups of three eighth-notes would be treated as triplets.

For He's a Jolly Good Fellow

Shaking

Harp players use *shaking* to add different types of decorations to a solo or accompaniment part. To shake a note or chord, simply move your harp quickly from side to side while playing. (Some players prefer to shake their heads back and forth to create the same effect.)

The symbol *tr* above the staff stands for *trill*. The wavy line following the trill symbol indicates that you shake back and forth continuously between these two-note chords.

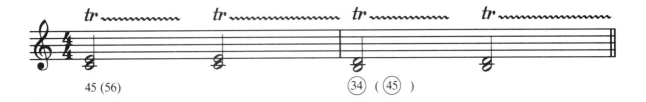

45 (56)   (34) ((45))

Now play "Red River Valley," using the trill shake where indicated.

Red River Valley

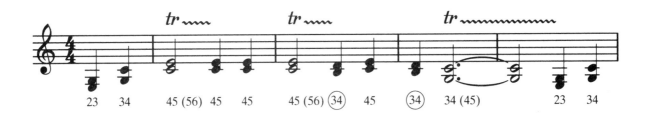

23   34   45 (56) 45   45   45 (56) (34) 45   (34) 34 (45)   23   34

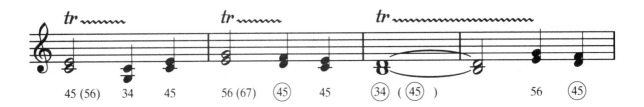

45 (56)   34   45   56 (67) (45) 45   (34) ((45))   56   (45)

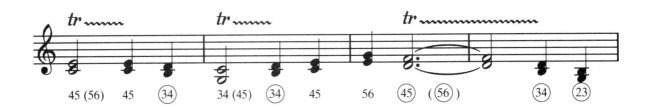

45 (56) 45 (34) 34 (45) (34) 45   56 (45) ((56))   (34) (23)

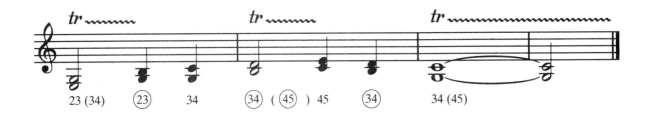

23 (34) (23) 34 (34) ((45)) 45 (34) 34 (45)

Tongue Blocking

As you may have already discovered, the tongue can be used to block airholes when they are not needed. Some harpists use *tongue blocking* frequently to achieve playing accuracy—particular in a single-note melody. Tongue blocking is also useful for "broken chord" playing. This jaunty, old-time playing style calls to mind the harmonica's other name, the *mouth organ*.

Place the right-hand corner of your mouth on airhole 5, and place your tongue gently over airholes 3 and 4.

Mouth Position for Tongue Blocking

The exercise that follows uses tongue blocking to create a broken chord accompaniment in the "oom-pah-pah" style. With your mouth and tongue in position, blow airhole 5 alone. While this note is sounding, lift and replace your tongue twice to play chords on airholes 3 and 4. This creates the classic "oom-pah-pah" rhythm. There's no need to move your mouth at all. Practice this tongue blocking exercise until you can play the broken chords with accuracy in tempo.

* = lift tongue

Now use this tongue blocking technique to play "The Irish Washerwoman" in broken chord style. Notice that all of the single-note passages are played with the tongue blocking the lower two notes.

The Irish Washerwoman

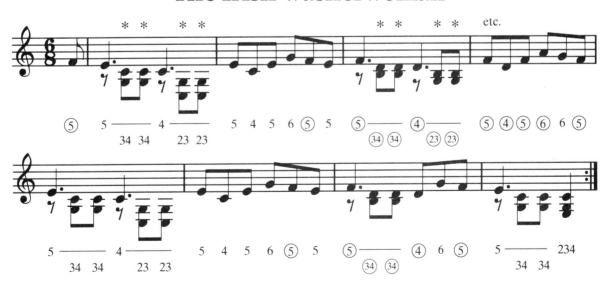

Syncopation

Syncopation is an important rhythmic technique which is widely used in jazz, blues, and rock music. Syncopated rhythms focus stress on beats that are not normally stressed in other forms of music. For example, a traditional folk song in ⁴₄ time features stress on the first and third beats of each measure, as in the first lines of "A-Tisket A-Tasket," shown below.

A jazz composition in ⁴₄ time often features syncopated notes and words just before or after the stressed beats of the music—on the *offbeats* of the rhythm. Ella Fitzgerald used this type of phrasing to achieve a swingy feel in "A-Tisket, A-Tasket," and created a jazz standard. Try playing this song with a syncopated jazz feel.

A-Tisket A-Tasket

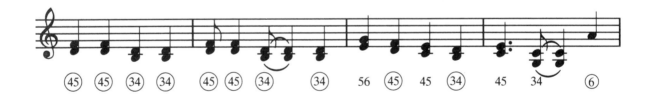

Note Bending

Note bending is an essential blues technique that opens up many new possibilities for the performer. Once you've got this technique under your belt, you'll be ready to do some serious blues jamming.

By bending a note downward, the player creates a new note one half-step lower. Follow these steps to bend a D note to a D♭ note.

- Place your mouth on airhole 1 and draw normally to play the D note. Now get ready to bend the note down to D♭.
- Purse and extend your lips. Allow your tongue to move toward the back of your mouth (as if you were whistling a low note).
- Intensify the flow of air drawn through airhole 1 as you tilt the instrument mouthpiece downward slightly.
- Make sure you are breathing from the diaphragm.

Practice bending the D note until you can move smoothly back and forth from D to D♭. Note that this bend is notated with an arrow (↓) beneath airhole 1.

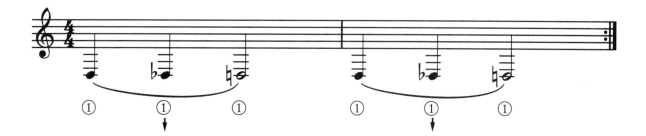

If you can't get this note to bend down right away, don't worry. Bending notes is a technique that you have to develop with practice. Bends are possible on all of the draw notes of holes 1 through 6. Try each one in turn, bending down and then releasing as shown. You will probably find some bends easier than others—and practicing these will help you get the feel for bending the more difficult notes.

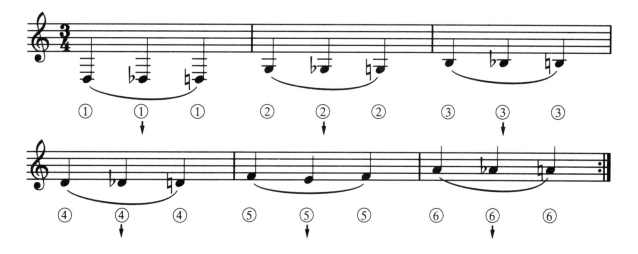

Now play Sloop John B., a West Indian folk song which became a favorite of the Beach Boys in 1966. Their recording of this classic tune stayed on the chart for ten weeks, topping at the third position. The steady rhythm and lilting melody of their recording made it a natural winner on the pop charts. Notice the bends in measures 7, 11, 14, 23, 27, and 30.

Sloop John B.

Crossharp

Most blues and rock solos are played using *crossharp* technique (also called *second position*). To play crossharp, you simply use a harmonica in the key five notes lower than the key of the song you are playing. In other words, if the song is in the key of G Major, you'll play a C harmonica. If the song is in D, you'd use an G harmonica, and so on. (See the "Key and Position Guide" at the end of the book for a complete listing of second-position keys.) If you're playing in a band, you'll eventually need to have harps in several keys. However, there's no need to rush out and purchase a harp in every key—you can get these harps as you need them. Since the harp you are using now is in the key of C, all the crossharp material that follows will be in the key of G.

The arrangement of "When the Saints Go Marching In" features both straight-harp and crossharp playing. Here's the pattern:

- The first verse of the song of the song is in the key of C (that's first-position or straight-harp style). This key is based on the C Major scale, which begins with the C note (blow airhole 4).
- The middle verse is in the key of G (second-position or crossharp style) in the high range of the harp. This key is based on the G Major scale, which begins with the G note (blow airhole 6).
- In the last verse, you'll get to play a variation of the crossharp part down an octave. In the low range, you can add some bluesy bends that bring out the New Orleans flavor of this old Dixieland favorite. Here, the G note is played as a draw on airhole 2.

As you play "When the Saints Go Marching In," observe the differences between the straight-harp and crossharp sounds. Practice this song until you are quite familiar with the different blow-and-draw patterns used in each verse.

When the Saints Go Marching In

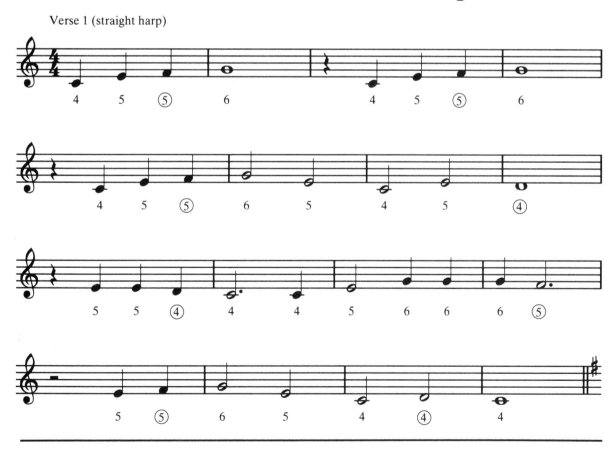

The Blues

The blues was born in the American South. It evolved from the work songs written by Black-American slaves before the Civil War—and so bears the influence of African rhythms and tonality. The blues is known for its power to evoke the listener's emotions—because its lyric often tells a personal story of troubles and longing. The plaintive melody and harmony of the blues, coupled with its strong and simple rhythm, make it a universally appealing musical form. Early blues masters quickly adapted the harmonica as a blues instrument. To this end, they created a range of new playing techniques which are still widely used by today's blues and rock harpists.

Most blues melodies and solos are based on the *pentatonic blues scale*. This scale has only five notes per octave (instead of seven, as found in the major scale). The *blue notes* are actually borrowed from the minor scale (which you'll learn in the next section). Playing these minor notes against the major blues chord progression gives the blues that dark and mournful sound. As you practice this blues scale, try to get a clear tone when you bend down on airhole 3 to play the B♭ note.

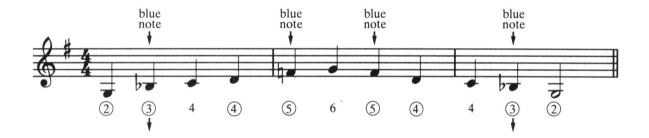

Many traditional blues songs and modern blues-rock tunes are written in *twelve-bar blues* form—with twelve bars (or measures) of music in each complete verse of the song. The vocal line is often stated in three phrases per verse (with four bars in each phrase). The repetition and simplicity of the twelve-bar blues form is the secret to its penetrating power and lasting popularity.

> Well, good morning blues, blues how do you do?
> Well, good morning blues, blues how do you do?
> Well, I'm doing all right, good morning, how are you?

Professional harpists know that a steady, driving rhythm and good breath control are what make a great performance. Your ability to bend notes with confidence will also give your playing a professional blues sound. Now play the melody line of "Good Morning Blues," a traditional favorite that has been recorded by many of the great blues masters.

Good Morning Blues

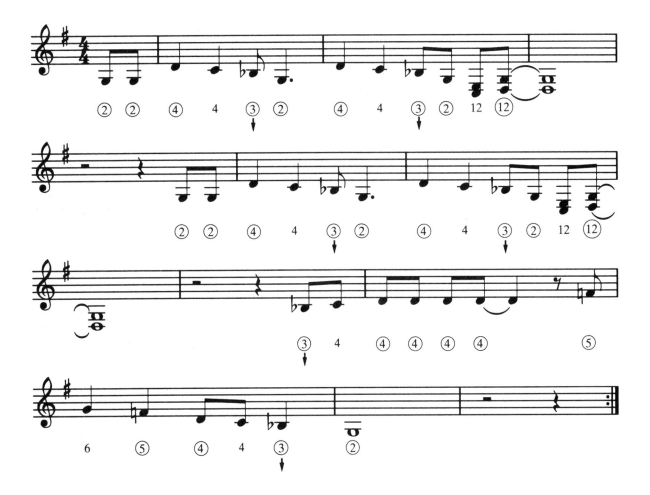

Blues Styles

Harpists use different basic playing styles to create backup and solo arrangements for songs. In the sections that follow, you'll learn the ins and outs of comping and soloing—and get some important tips on which style to use for a given song.

Comping and Fills

The term *comping* is short for "accompaniment." For this style, the harpist plays a chorded backup or *rhythm part* while another instrument or a vocalist carries the tune. To make comping interesting, harpists often add bluesy riffs in between selected lines of the song. These riffs are called *fills* because they "fill in" the space between phrases of the song—and lead the ear back to each new line of the melody. Use comping and fills when you play with a singer—or when someone else in the band is taking a solo.

Take a look at "C.C. Rider," an all-time favorite blues and rock hit that has been performed by a range of artists. Ma Rainey brought this tune to position fourteen on the charts in 1925. In 1957, rhythm and blues singer Chuck Willis had a career-making hit with this song—and inspired the dance craze called "The Stroll." In 1963, rhythm and blues singer LaVern Baker recorded her hit version of this tune (entitled "See See Rider"). The magic had still not worn off this terrific rhythm number—for Eric Burdon & the Animals made "See See Rider" a hit once again for seven weeks in 1966. Use comping and fills to play this song—and add a few bluesy shakes and bends in the third phrase for variety.

C.C. Rider

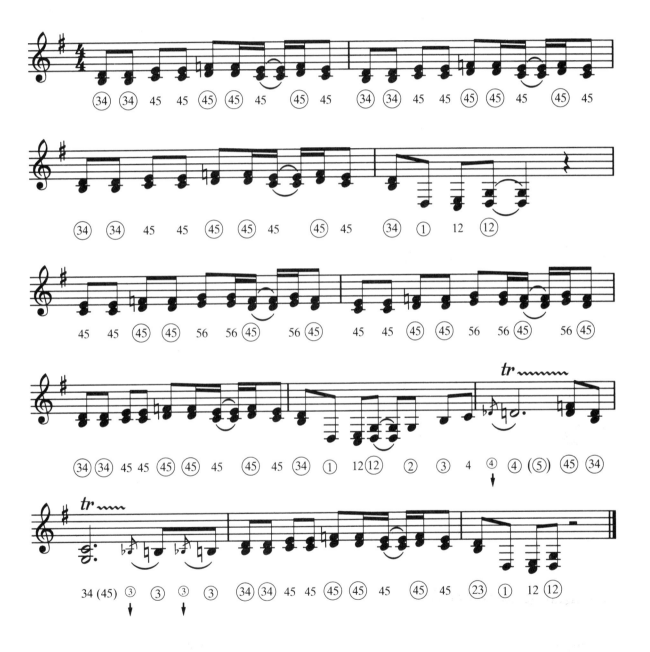

Soloing

Soloing is an important part of harmonica playing. Most of the tunes you have learned so far have been solos. When you play a solo, you can either play the melody or a variation that fits in with the chord progression. In this section, you will get to do both.

"Frankie and Johnny" is perhaps the most famous blues of all time. This stark tale of love and murder was recorded by many great blues artists—and was a signature tune for Mae West. As a testament to this song's versatility, R&B singer-songwriter Brook Benton put it on the charts for four weeks in 1961; soul singer Sam Cooke put it on the charts for seven weeks in 1963; and Elvis Presley, the king of rock and roll, made it a hit once again for five weeks in 1966.

The first time through, play the melody—the second time, play the solo variation as written. Notice how the solo makes use of repeated riffs and the outlining of chord tones to produce a natural sounding melody that is completely different from the real melody of the song.

Frankie and Johnny

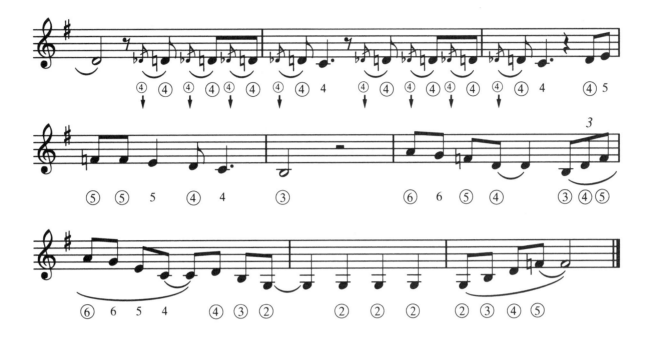

Blues Effects

Blues players use a number of special effects to make the harp "talk." By changing the shape and position of the mouth, lips, tongue, and hands, you can add character to your own blues solos—and create some interesting riffs. In the sections that follow, you'll learn some classic effects like wah-wah, throat popping, and train sounds. These will come in handy when you begin to improvise your own blues harp solos, or jam with a band.

Wah-Wah

Wah-wah is a bending technique which is widely used by all blues and rock harpists. Folk musicians first invented this sound as an imitation of a train whistle. (You'll get to use the wah-wah in this way in the next section "Train Sounds.") Follow these steps to play the wah-wah exercise below:

- Cover the sound holes of the harp from behind with your right hand (as you learned in the section "Vibrato"). Form your mouth and tongue as if you were saying "oo," and bend the C♯ note on airhole 4.
- As you continue to draw on this airhole, release the bend and form your mouth into an "ah" shape. At the same time, uncover the harp's sound holes with your right hand.
- Repeat the previous steps in tempo.

  Practice this "wah-wah" until you can play it smoothly and evenly.

The wah-wah effect adds a down-and-dirty sound to this classic boogie rock blues. You may want to even add a little growl to your wah-wah by vibrating the back of your throat lightly as you inhale (like a little snore). Just cover two airholes when you play the two-note wah-wah in the first line. Also, remember to use your right hand as a mute to bring out the bluesy wah-wah sound.

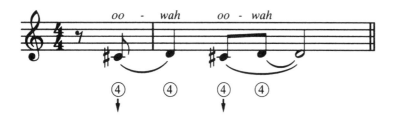

Boogie Rock Blues

Train Sounds

The early blues masters were travelling musicians, migrant workers, and hoboes. It's not surprising that the train appears in many early blues songs and spirituals as a symbol of hope and freedom. The harmonica is famous for its ability to produce unusual sound effects—especially the "chugga-chugga" and lonesome whistle of an old-time steam locomotive. The wah-wah effect that you learned in the previous section makes an ideal train whistle. The chugging sound of the engine is produced using quickly tongued chords in a rhythmic blow/draw pattern. As you practice this chugging pattern, breath directly from the diaphragm (as if you are panting after a short sprint). Lightly whisper the words "too-koo" as you double tongue each chord. (The music has been written up an octave to make it easier to read.)

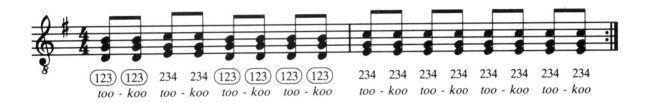

Here another interesting chugging pattern for you to try. Mastering the tonguing and slurring to this pattern is a bit like learning to say a tongue twister—start out slowly and increase the tempo gradually, like a train building up speed.

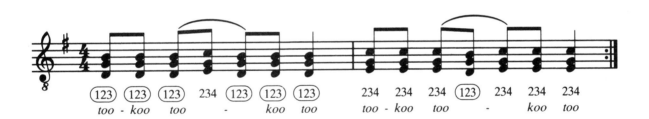

Now take a look at "Rock Island Line" which uses two different chugging patterns and a few well-placed wah-wahs to produce an exciting train effect. This traditional train song became a top-10 hit for Lonnie Donegan in 1956. Practice "Rock Island Line" until you can play it accurately in rhythm. Controlled deep breathing is key to playing this song with power and stamina.

Rock Island Line

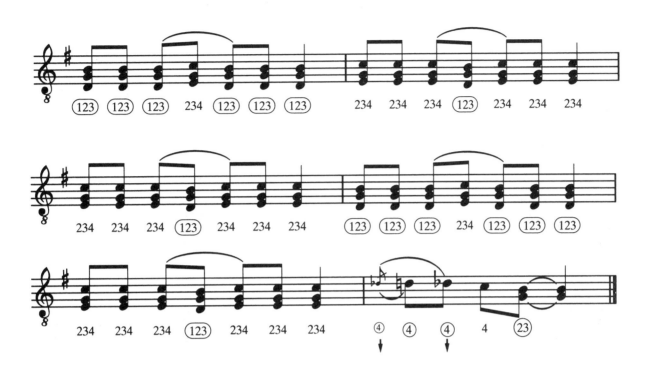

Throat Popping

Blues harpists use *throat popping* to add a sharp, percussive attack to selected notes of a song. To create this effect, start each chord with an explosive "ka" sound in the very back of your throat.

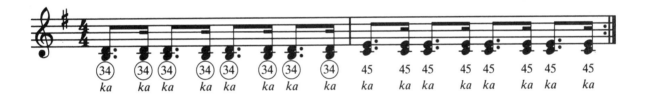

Throat popping is especially useful when you want to play bent notes, because the sharp attack helps force the bend down. This means that you can begin by playing a bent note, then release the bend to play the natural draw note on the same airhole. Use using throat popping throughout the song "Wimoweh." This traditional South African Zulu song (retitled "The Lion Sleeps Tonight") became a number one hit for the Tokens (featuring Neil Sedaka) in 1961. Robert John put it back on the charts for 13 weeks in 1972. Notice how throat popping helps accent the bouncy rhythm of this song. Remember to use the "ka" sound to attack the bends in measures 4, 8, and 10.

Wimoweh

Improvising a Blues Solo

So far, you have played solo on many song melodies. You've learned to create melody variations and to play riffs to fill in between the lines of a song. The next section provides a variety of blues and rock riffs that you can use when writing your own harp solos. *Improvising* is an important solo style used in today's blues, rock, and country music. From this point on, you'll probably want to devote some extra practice time to this exciting playing style—particularly if you plan to play with a band. The next section also provides some helpful tips on building a solo—and shows you how to use turnarounds and endings effectively. As you practice improvising, feel free to explore the techniques and special effects you have learned so far—and take the time to develop your own riffs and variations.

Blues Riffs

Riffs are the building blocks of improvisation—so it really pays to have quite a few to choose from when you begin improvising. First, take a look at the chord progression used in a standard twelve-bar blues song. Notice that the verse is made up of three lines of equal length.

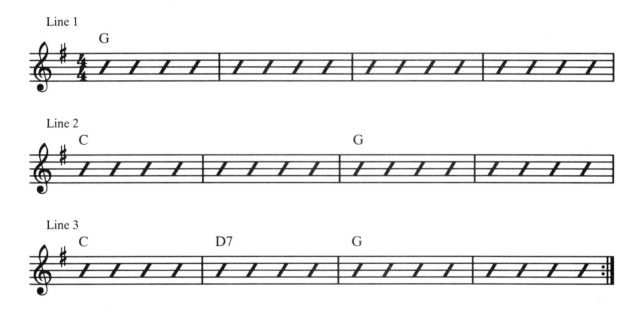

Some riffs work best with the first and second lines of a blues progression. Others are designed for the third line or ending riff of a blues song—and often include a *turnaround* in the last two measures. A turnaround is any kind of fill that leads nicely back to the beginning of the verse—or prepares the song's ending. Practice these riffs until you can play each of them from memory.

First and Second Line Riffs

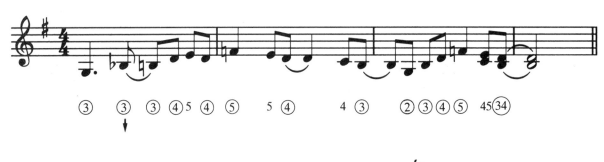

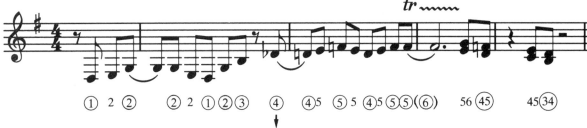

Third Line Riffs

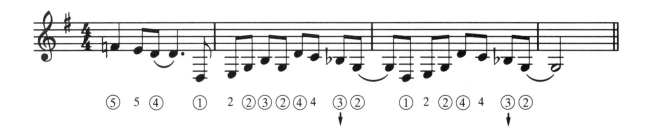

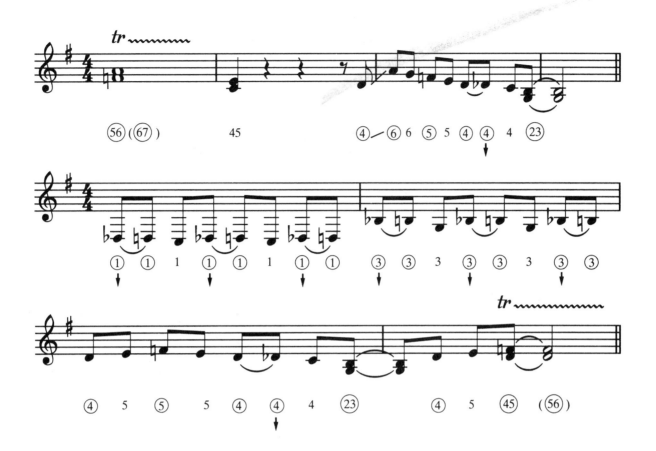

As you practice improvising solos, you will discover many more riffs of your own. Decide which lines each riff works best with, memorize it, and write it down in a notebook for future reference.

Now get ready to improvise on a rock-blues version of "Crossroads," a traditional tune that Cream turned into a rock and roll hit in 1969. Originally entitled "Crossroad Blues," this song was a favorite of blues master Robert Johnson. Play the melody the first time through, then follow these steps to create two solo verses.

• Choose a riff for the first line of your solo.
• Repeat the riff in the second line.
• Play a third-line riff, then get ready to repeat the verse.
• Choose a new first-line verse for your second solo verse.
• Try a variation of this riff in the second line.
• Play a new third-line riff to end the solo.

Crossroads

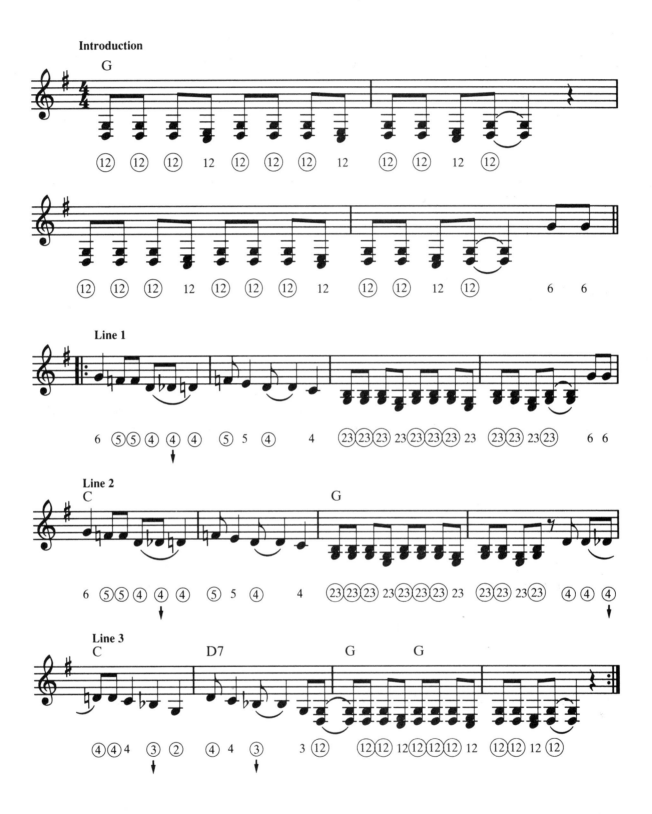

Third Position

So far, you have played straight-harp songs in the key of C Major and crossharp songs in the key of G Major. In this section, you'll learn to play songs in *D Minor* by playing in *third position*. Songs written in a minor key often have a dark, introspective, or sad quality. In this position, you use a harmonica one whole-step lower than the key of the song you wish to play. In other words, if the song is in the key of D Minor, you'll play a C harmonica. If the song is in E Minor, you'd use a D harmonica, and so on. (See the "Key and Position Guide" at the end of the book for a complete listing of third-position keys.)

The minor scale is formed by lowering certain notes of the corresponding major scale (usually the third, sixth, and seventh scale degrees). Play the third-position minor scale—D Minor—beginning with a draw note on airhole 4.

Take a look at the Simon & Garfunkel hit "Scarborough Fair," shown here in the key of D Minor. This popular folk song is easy to play—and sounds great on a C harmonica in third position.

Scarborough Fair

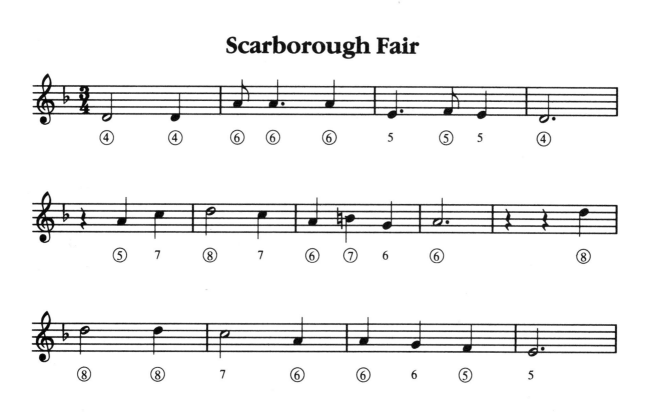

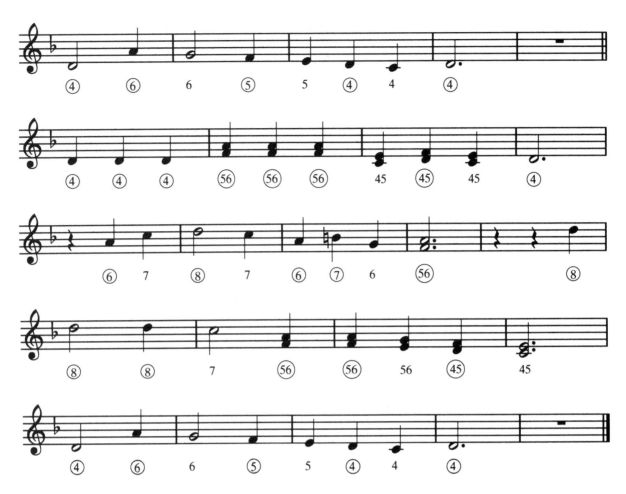

Minor Blues

So far, you've played blues songs in the key of G Major using the G pentatonic blues scale in second position. In third position, you can play minor blues songs in the key of D Minor using the D pentatonic blues scale. You can play this blues scale without bending any notes.

Now get ready to play a blues version of "The House of the Rising Sun," which is written here in the key of D Minor. This hard-driving ballad was a number one hit for the Animals in 1964—then Frijid Pink put it on the charts again for eleven weeks in 1970. The D Minor scale and chord progression gives "House of the Rising Sun" a raw and powerful sound—and sets the stage for the song's tragic message. A few selected bends on airholes 4, 5, and 6 create the overall bluesy effect. Play the melody the first time through, then play the solo verse as written. After you have learned these, improvise your own two-verse solo. Feel free to explore the techniques and special effects you already know using the D pentatonic blues scale and the D Minor scale—and take the time to develop your own riffs and variations.

House of the Rising Sun

Using the Microphone

Since the harp is an *acoustic* (or non-electric) instrument, it is almost always amplified in performance. If you are planning to play in a blues or rock band—or record your playing—it's a good idea to get some practice working with a microphone first. Here are tips that will help you develop and perfect your microphone technique.

• Adjust the microphone stand to a comfortable height. If you are sharing a mike with another instrumentalist or vocalist, adjust the microphone to a height that is most suitable for both of you. When it's your turn at the mike, simply pivot the microphone up or down if you need to further adjust the playing height. (Also, remember to step aside after your solo or featured section. This small consideration can impress fellow musicians even more than the showiest harp solo.)

• Keep your instrument very close to the microphone. If you hear any crackling, squealing, or other feedback, you are too close—or your amplifier volume needs to be turned down. If you can not hear yourself, you're either too far away from the mike—or your amplifier volume needs to be turned up.

• Many blues and rock players do not use a microphone stand. Instead, they cup the microphone in the same hand used to hold the instrument. This technique takes a little practice, but helps give the player a great deal of power and control—to the point where the mike actually becomes a part of the instrument. For this style, it's important to use a microphone that is small and light. You'll also want to be sure that the microphone is *unidirectional* to keep feedback to a minimum. It also helps if you use a *dynamic* or *ribbon* microphone to prevent distortion.

• A long, high-quality microphone cord will give you freedom of movement on stage. A *coiled* cord will help prevent annoying tangles.

• If you plan to perform regularly with a microphone, you may want to consider getting a small amplifier of your own. (A good-quality 60 to 80 watt amp is adequate for most performance situations.) This will give you control over the volume, tone, and reverb of your sound—and allow you to perform consistently well on familiar equipment. If you do not have your own amp—or if you are performing in a large club—you'll plug directly in to a PA system. The sound engineer will control your volume, tone, and reverb settings—and you'll be able to hear your performance through monitor speakers.

• There are a wide variety of microphones, amplifiers, and sound systems in use. It pays to experiment with different set-ups—and learn how to make the equipment bring out the best in your playing. Good microphone technique is almost as important as good playing, so practice whenever you can—and be on the lookout for opportunities to perform and record.

Key and Position Chart

This chart will help you figure out which key harmonica to use when playing in second or third position. You can locate the key of your harmonica in the first column—this is the key stamped on the harp—and read across to find out what keys you can play in using the other two positions. If you know the key and position in which you want to play, the chart will tell you what key harmonica you need. Notice that certain keys may have more than one name, such as A♯, which is the same as B♭.

First-Position (Straight-Harp) Key	Second-Position (Crossharp) Key	Third-Position Key
A	E	B Minor
A♯/B♭	F	C Minor
B	F♯/G♭	C♯/D♭ Minor
C	G	D Minor
C♯/D♭	G♯/A♭	D♯/E♭ Minor
D	A	E Minor
D♯/E♭	A♯/B♭	F Minor
E	B	F♯/G♭ Minor
F	C	G Minor
F♯/G♭	C♯/D♭	G♯/A♭ Minor
G	D	A Minor
G♯/A♭	D♯/E♭	A♯/B♭ Minor

Further Study

Congratulations! You have completed a comprehensive course in harmonica that will provide a broad foundation for your continued development of your harmonica skills and personal playing style. From this point on, you'll be busy exploring the melodies of your favorite songs, as well as ones that are unfamiliar to you.

As you develop your repertoire, you may want to get together for sessions with friends who sing or play other instruments. Listen to recordings of different harp players—and practice the riffs and techniques used in their solo and accompaniment parts. Here are a few suggestions:

Urban Blues: Little Walter, Rice Miller, Big Walter Horton, Junior Wells, James Cotton, Four City Joe, Paul Butterfield

Country Blues: Sonny Terry, Sonny Boy Williamson

Country: Charlie McCoy, Mickey Raphael

Jazz: Toots Thielemans

Pop: Stevie Wonder, Norton Buffalo

Rock: Bruce Springsteen

Folk: Bob Dylan

At this point, you have all the facts you need to continue your development as a knowledgable and competent harpist. Music and record stores and libraries will now provide you with many new doorways to a lifetime of playing enjoyment.